Contents

Acknowledgments ii
Foreword 1
History of Kew Gardens 2
History of postcards 5
Postcard messages 8
Map of Kew Gardens 10

The postcards
The gates 12
The Orangery 14
Kew Palace 16
The Temple of the Sun 19
Stone Pine 20
Cambridge Cottage 21
The Rock Garden 22
The Rose Pergola 24
T-Range glasshouses 25
Victoria amazonica 27
Princess of Wales Conservatory 28
The Temple of Aeolus 29
The Museum 30
The Palm House 33
The Rose Garden 37
The Rhododendron Dell 38
The Lake and the Lily Pond 40
The Queen's Cottage 43
The Japanese Gateway 46
The Pagoda 47
The Restaurant and the Ruined Arch 50
The Marianne North Gallery 52
The Flagstaff 55
The Temperate House 56
King William's Temple 58
The Herbarium 58
Spring flowers 60
Plant portraits 63
Kew 66
Kew Bridge and the Thames 68

Appendix — postcard publishers 72
References 72

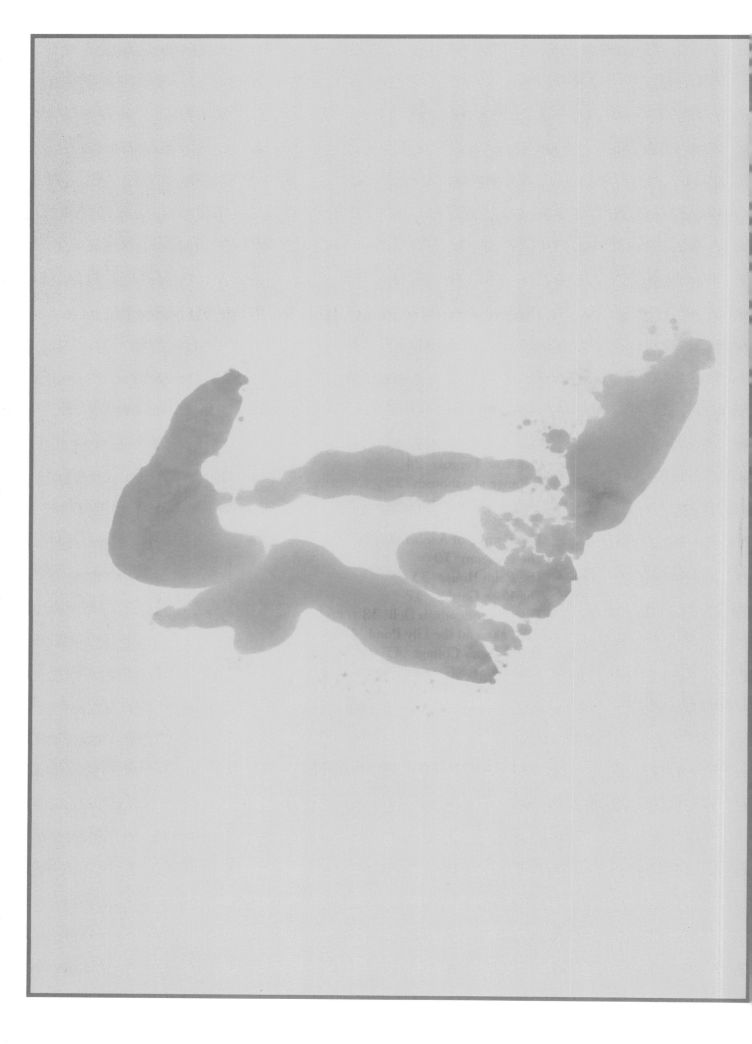

Foreword

Ten years ago I could not resist buying a collection of some 50 Kew cards chanced upon while browsing in a local bookshop. A search through the illustrations in the Kewensia collection of Kew Library revealed many more Kew postcards and I was hooked—I visited bookshops, antiques fairs, junk shops and especially the larger monthly and annual postcard sales in London. In the early days even the rarer cards were available for 20 or 30 pence but as my collection grew and word got around prices escalated! One or two other staff members in the gardens had been purchasing Kew cards and one of the best collections was built up by Phillip Cribb, who magnanimously donated his whole album to me. Friends abroad started to search for cards and donated them to my collection; beautiful cards arrived from America and France. Dealers sent me cards for sale and I wrote to all the publishers known to have produced Kew cards. This further excited my interest, as several firms were no longer in business and a few, including the famous Raphael Tuck and Sons, had lost most of their archives during the World War 2 bombing and retained no records of what they had printed. My search became a detective operation rewarding me with great pleasure each time I discovered the last card of a numbered set.

The 119 cards selected for this book represent approximately an eighth of my collection and were chosen to show a range of features throughout the gardens. In conjunction with the map the book offers an alternative illustrated guide to Kew. The postcards, ranging from Victorian to present day, are a pictorial document of some of the changes in the gardens over the last 90 years. A few of the buildings featured are no longer standing, having been either destroyed by natural catastrophe, such as the Temple of the Sun, or replaced by modern equivalents, like the magnificent Princess of Wales Conservatory, which replaced the 'T-range' glasshouses.

History of Kew Gardens

The Royal Botanic Gardens, Kew, date from about 1730 when George II and Queen Caroline took possession of Richmond Lodge, and their son Frederick, Prince of Wales, acquired Kew House (or the White House). Both residences have since been demolished. In 1759 Frederick's widow Augusta, Dowager Princess of Wales, created a small botanic garden of nine acres on land south of the Orangery.

It was during the reign of George III, who succeeded his grandfather in 1760, that the Richmond and Kew estates were joined and the botanic garden became famous, largely due to the efforts of the unofficial director, Sir Joseph Banks, and the head gardener, William Aiton. Architecturally the gardens were distinguished by the work of Sir William Chambers, born in Sweden in 1723, who between 1757 and 1762 designed and executed some two dozen miscellaneous buildings of which only six survive today. Four are illustrated in this book: the Pagoda, Orangery, Ruined Arch and Temple of Aeolus (the latter rebuilt in 1845).

In 1841, the small botanic garden was acquired by the nation, and the first director, Sir William Hooker, increased the size of the gardens to over 250 acres and established the Herbarium and Library and the Museum of Economic Botany. Queen's Cottage and its grounds were given to the gardens in 1897 on the occasion of Queen Victoria's Diamond Jubilee, and the land around Kew Palace a few years later. Cambridge Cottage was presented to Kew by King Edward VII on the death of the last Duke of Cambridge in 1904.

The gardens have suffered several disasters both from natural causes and the activities of man — or more specifically, in one

Clockwise: an 1888 engraving of the Refreshment Pavilion; its charred remains after suffragettes set fire to it in 1913; the remnants of a light aircraft that crashed in the gardens in August 1928; the plane that made a forced landing near Victoria Gate in January 1938; and the end of the Temple of the Sun, demolished by a cedar of Lebanon during a storm on 28 March 1916.

3

instance, women! On a February morning in 1913 two suffragettes burnt down the Refreshment Pavilion, which was later replaced in 1915. During the Second World War more than 30 bombs and hundreds of incendiaries fell on Kew but inflicted little damage. One light aircraft crashed in the gardens on 16 August 1928 and another made a forced landing on the lawn near Victoria Gate on 5 January 1938 — and most staff would be happier if Concorde's flight path was not directly over Kew. On 3 August 1879 a great hailstorm broke nearly 40,000 panes of greenhouse glass and over 100 years later the great storm of 16 October 1987 destroyed hundreds of trees, many of them irreplaceable. (Kew's sister garden at Wakehurst Place in Sussex lost an estimated 15-20,000 trees.) The Temple of the Sun was destroyed during a less violent storm on 28 March 1916, when a cedar of Lebanon fell and demolished it.

The last decade has witnessed a proliferation of new buildings at Kew and several of the glasshouses have been completely renovated or replaced. The new Centre of Economic Botany (the Sir Joseph Banks Building) highlights a return to the important study of plant uses, and the Princess of Wales Conservatory, with its computer-controlled climates (from desert to cloud forest), will stand as a landmark of architectural and technological development as Kew enters the 21st century.

From 31 March 1903 until 1 April 1984 Kew was under the administrative control of the Ministry of Agriculture, Fisheries and Food (originally the Board of Agriculture) but since then has been controlled by a Board of Trustees. Kew is a scientific institution of international repute and houses an unrivalled collection of plants and plant material which, together with the library, provides the raw material for research in several fields of botany.

History of postcards

On 1 October 1869 the Austrian postal service issued the world's first postcard—the 'Correspondenz-Karte'. Although various cards had been posted before then, the cost of transmission had been the same as for letters, but these new postcards were sent at half letter-rate, a ploy designed to stimulate the business of the Austrian Post Office. The British and Swiss post offices issued their first postcards exactly one year later and other countries quickly followed, Canada in 1871, America and France in 1873 and Italy in 1874. British postcards were simply rectangles of buff-coloured card overprinted with the new halfpenny violet Queen Victoria stamp. These cards could only be purchased from post offices and the General Post Office had given sole printing rights to the printers De La Rue, so the government held a tightly controlled monopoly on their production. At first, transmission of postcards was restricted to within the issuing country, but the Universal Postal Union soon negotiated international use.

The postcards were handled by many people between sender and recipient, and the tourist industry, in particular, was quick to realise the vast advertising potential. Several firms began printing their advertising slogans or associated line drawings on the official postcards and the era of the picture postcard had arrived. In 1872 British printers persuaded the Post Office to authorise production of the first private postcards, thus permitting British firms to catch up with their continental competitors. But the card size was still governed by the Post Office (122×88mm or 121×74mm) and illustrations had to share the front of the card with necessarily brief written messages, while the back was reserved solely for the address. Pictures were consequently rather small and often took the form of vignettes covering only a portion of the front of the card. Soon the French, British and then Germans were producing finely illustrated cards, and some of the earliest postcards of Kew were printed in Germany using their photolitho printing techniques developed in 1892.

On 1 November 1899 an increase in size of the privately printed postcard (to 140 × 89mm) was permitted and, with advance knowledge of this, Raphael Tuck & Sons were able to launch their first designs on the very same day. Another significant date in the development of the picture postcard was 1902, when the German-born F Hartmann, having set up a postcard publishing business in Britain, developed the idea of dividing the back of the card into two — one side for the message, the other for the address — leaving the whole of the front for the illustration. Within four years this idea had been accepted by all Universal Postal Union members and the postcard boom began.

As printing techniques changed so the style of postcards altered, but some of the early cards of Kew are undoubtedly the most beautiful. Photographic cards were often hand-tinted or colourwashed, and some elegant glossy sepia photographs were issued in the Edwardian era by Gale & Polden Ltd of London, Aldershot and Portsmouth. By 1903 Raphael Tuck & Sons had already launched their famous 'Oilette' series with their internationally recognised symbol of artists' easel and palette. Tuck Oilettes, reproduced from original paintings, were usually sold in packages of six cards, each identified by its own number to assist collectors and encourage the collecting trend. At least three sets of Kew were produced but I have been unsuccessful in tracing all eighteen cards, and as Tuck's archives were largely destroyed during the Second World War I have no way of knowing what pictures I am looking for. Examples of Tuck Oilettes included in this book, painted mainly by anonymous artists, are cards 3, 15, 27, 37, 71, 93, 94, 116 and 117. 'Kew Gardens in Springtime', cards 93 and 94, were both painted by M Townsend and card 116 (Kew Bridge) was by Walter Hayward-Young, or 'Jotter' as he was universally known.

J Salmon of Sevenoaks in Kent also produced many post-cards of Kew, and their reproductions of watercolour paintings by the artist C T Howard (cards 21, 42, 50, 52, 56, 64, 68 & 85) are some of the most appealing.

As well as producing sepia photographic cards of Kew, Gale & Polden Ltd also commissioned Robert Hughes to paint watercolour scenes. One of my favourites is his rendering of the Rhododendron Dell (card 54) which epitomises the gardens in May and is used as the centrepiece on the front cover of this book. Other cards by Hughes are numbers 19, 24, 35, 65 and 73.

Some well-known photographers occasionally chose Kew as their subject. Card 62, a photograph of the Queen's Cottage, was taken early this century by the French photographer who signed himself simply 'L.L.' Although he is known in many parts of the world for the quality of his work, speculation remains as to his true identity. Dûval and Monahan, however, in *Collecting Postcards in Colour, 1894-1914,* showed after a little detective work that LL was probably Louis Levy.

Since 1900 many publishing houses have issued postcards of Kew. Only a few of these companies are still in operation and even fewer still produce postcards. An appendix lists the 23 firms who printed most of the 119 cards illustrated.

Postcard messages

Since the turn of the century postcards have been sent to
friends at home and abroad. During the late Victorian
and early Edwardian eras and during both world wars mil-
lions of postcards with messages of love, hope, con-
gratulation and sympathy were posted. With the efficient
postal service and, in England, two or even three deliveries
per day the postcard was one of the quickest and cheapest
means of communication before the widespread introduc-
tion of the telephone. People actually sent postcards from
Kew in the morning informing a mother, sister or aunt that
they would arrive in Hampstead or even Brighton for tea that
same afternoon! Postcards were widely used to send birth-
day greetings, as get-well cards, as short love letters and
simply to keep in touch. As the number and diversity of the
cards increased a collecting boom began and cards were
often sent solely for their aesthetic appeal. Famous artists
were employed to paint anything and everything and some of
the most beautiful cards of Kew are paintings commissioned
by the larger and better-known postcard printers. 'Isn't this a
pretty picture?' became a favourite oneliner on cards sent to
fellow collectors. 'Many thanks for pretty P.C., I have 315
now' and 'Another — sweetheart, for your collection. Writing
you tomorrow, so good night. Best love and kisses. From
yours ever' were more personal messages on two Kew cards
in my collection. Every now and then extraordinary messages add amusement to postcard collecting: 'Do not come
home until I tell you as we are having hot water put in and all
is confusion' or 'the essence of ginger is for indigestion, I
ought to have explained', or even 'I shall be unable to come
tonight, because I have to go to Ipswich with some gentle-
man'.

One or two companies produced postcards of Kew in sets of
six and in some cases all six were evidently sent to the same

person with a running message. I would dearly like to know what was written on the other cards of a Tuck series of which I have only card 3, announcing 'we have got a yard of liv. sausage waiting for your return'. And then there is the romantic note: 'Is it to be the same place and the same time tomorrow evening?' or 'I think I should like married life if it was like this card, wouldn't you?' And of course there is always the English weather: 'We had summer on Monday and winter today!'

Some authors thoughtfully recorded historical events at Kew or details of some of the buildings. A postcard of the Temple of the Sun posted at Kew on 24 April 1916 says 'Just a card to show the temple that was destroyed in the gale'. Another enchanting message on the back of a view of the Palm House reads 'This is one of the largest houses in Kew Gardens dearie. In the centre is such a lovely large palm up to the roof. There is a spiral staircase to go up almost to the top, it is a pretty sight to look down on all the different kinds. You would like to see them dearie, but it is hot in these houses, a clammy heat'. During the Second World War some Kew postcards had printed messages from the Prime Minister on the reverse. One example, on a card printed by J Salmon Ltd, quoted 'We have to gain the Victory. That is our task'.

Whatever the message there can be little doubt that the receipt of a postcard brightens up the day and shows that someone somewhere is thinking about *you*.

Map

Numbers on the map refer to the postcards illustrated in this book

*Buildings that have been destroyed or replaced: 14-16, 25, 26, 27-30

Cards not on map: 59, 93, 95, 96, 98, 99, 100-107, 113-119

━━━ Possible route round gardens

Royal Botanic Gardens Kew

Guides, Picture Postcards and Publications may be purchased at the Bookshop (Orangery) F1

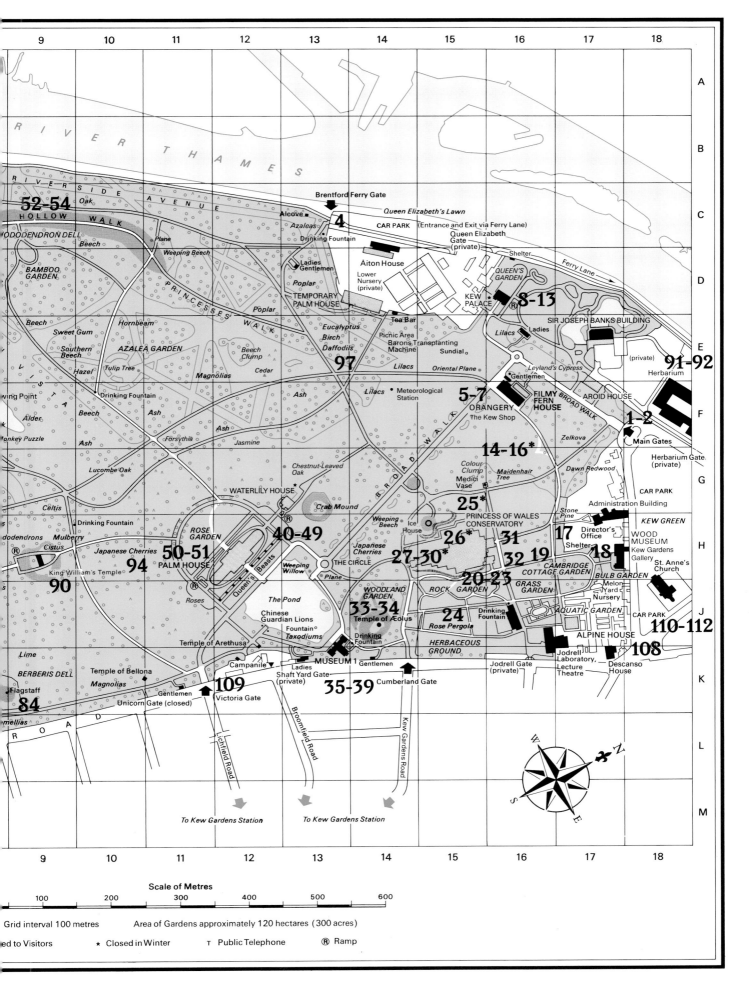

52-54
RIVER THAMES
RIVER SIDE AVENUE
HOLLOW WALK
RHODODENDRON DELL
Oak
Alcove
Azaleas
Drinking Fountain
Brentford Ferry Gate
Queen Elizabeth's Lawn
4
CAR PARK (Entrance and Exit via Ferry Lane)
Queen Elizabeth Gate (private)
Shelter
Ferry Lane

BAMBOO GARDEN
Plane
Weeping Beech
Beech
Ladies
Gentlemen
Poplar
Aiton House
Lower Nursery (private)
QUEEN'S GARDEN
KEW PALACE
Ⓡ **8-13**
SIR JOSEPH BANKS BUILDING
Lilacs
Ladies
(private)
91-92
Herbarium

Beech
Sweet Gum
Southern Beech
Hornbeam
Hazel
Tulip Tree
PRINCESSES' WALK
AZALEA GARDEN
Magnolias
Beech Clump
Cedar
TEMPORARY PALM HOUSE
Eucalyptus
Birch
Daffodils
97
Tea Bar
Picnic Area
Barons Transplanting Machine
Sundial
Lilacs
Oriental Plane
Leyland's Cypress
Gentlemen
5-7
ORANGERY
FILMY FERN HOUSE
AROID HOUSE
1-2
Main Gates
Herbarium Gate (private)

Drinking Fountain
Beech
Ash
Ash
Forsythia
Jasmine
Lilacs
Meteorological Station
The Kew Shop
Zelkova
VISTA
Alder
Monkey Puzzle
Ash
14-16*
Colour Clump
Medici Vase
Maidenhair Tree
Dawn Redwood
BROAD WALK
Viewing Point

Lucombe Oak
Chestnut-Leaved Oak
WATERLILY HOUSE *
Crab Mound
25*
Stone Pine
Administration Building
CAR PARK
Celtis
Drinking Fountain
Weeping Beech
Ice House
PRINCESS OF WALES CONSERVATORY
26*
31
17
Director's Office
Shelter
KEW GREEN
WOOD MUSEUM
Kew Gardens Gallery
St. Anne's Church

dodendrons
Mulberry
Cistus
ROSE GARDEN
Ⓡ **40-49**
THE CIRCLE
Japanese Cherries
27-30*
32 19
18
CAMBRIDGE COTTAGE GARDEN
GRASS GARDEN
BULB GARDEN
Melon Yard Nursery
AQUATIC GARDEN
CAR PARK

King William's Temple
Japanese Cherries
50-51
PALM HOUSE
94
Queen's Beasts
Weeping Willow
Plane
Japanese Cherries
ROCK GARDEN
20-23
90
Roses
WOODLAND GARDEN
33-34
Temple of Aeolus
24
Rose Pergola
Drinking Fountain
ALPINE HOUSE
110-112

Lime
BERBERIS DELL
Temple of Arethusa
The Pond
Chinese Guardian Lions
Fountain
Taxodiums
HERBACEOUS GROUND
Jodrell Laboratory, Lecture Theatre
Descanso House
108

Flagstaff
84
Magnolias
Temple of Bellona
Campanile
Ladies
Shaft Yard Gate (private)
MUSEUM 1
Gentlemen
Jodrell Gate (private)
Camellias
Gentlemen
Unicorn Gate (closed)
109
Victoria Gate
35-39
Cumberland Gate
ROAD
Lichfield Road
Broomfield Road
Kew Gardens Road

To Kew Gardens Station
To Kew Gardens Station

Scale of Metres
100   200   300   400   500   600

Grid interval 100 metres   Area of Gardens approximately 120 hectares (300 acres)

ed to Visitors   ★ Closed in Winter   ⊤ Public Telephone   Ⓡ Ramp

The gates

Most visitors enter the gardens by the main gates off Kew Green. These were designed by Decimus Burton and erected in 1845, slightly to the west of the former main entrance which had a lion and unicorn on two large piers. These beasts now top two gates bearing their names on Kew Road (Unicorn gate is not open to the public). When English currency went decimal in 1971 the entrance charge to Kew was one of the few things that dropped in price—from three old pence to one new one. The charge has slowly risen to help pay for the running of the gardens—but Kew is still wonderful value for money.

Of the nine gates around the perimeter of the gardens only five are presently open to the public—the main gates (cards 1 and 2); Brentford Ferry Gate (4); Victoria Gate (109), the most convenient for visitors arriving at Kew underground station; Cumberland Gate; and Lion Gate (3), which is fifteen minutes walk from Richmond railway station and gives immediate views of the famous Pagoda.

1   Principal Entrance, Kew Gardens.

2

3

4

The Orangery

The Orangery has changed functions more times than any other Kew building. It was built in 1761 for Princess Augusta to the design of Sir William Chambers, and although apparently of stone it is actually a brick structure covered with a durable form of stucco made to look like stone. Originally known simply as the Greenhouse, it housed other plants in addition to oranges, and in 1841 most of the orange trees, which had never really flourished, were sent to Kensington Palace. Later it was used to display a magnificent collection of timbers from the Great Exhibition of 1862 and became known as Museum No 3 or the Wood Museum until 1958 (6 and 5). In 1959, after sensitive classical restyling and the addition of some Renaissance statues, the building was reopened by Her Majesty the Queen, once again as an orangery. The following year extensive dry rot was discovered and the building was closed for major repair work. It reopened as an exhibition centre and shop, a function that it still serves today.

TRADE MARK
ILLUSTRATED

'Misch & Co.'s "Camera Graphs". Series No. 616/5'

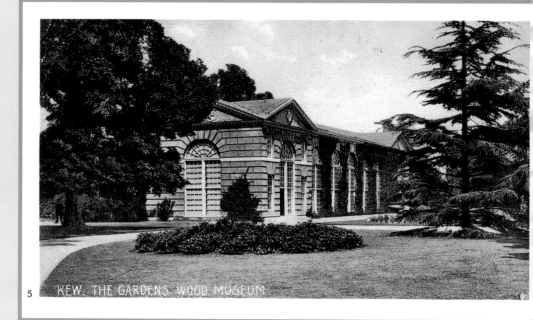

5 KEW. THE GARDENS WOOD MUSEUM

LONDON. MUSEUM Nº 3., KEW GARDENS.

6

7

Kew Palace

Kew Palace, originally known as the Dutch House because of its style and origin, was built in 1631 by a Dutch merchant named Samuel Fortney. It was erected upon the foundations of an old dwelling called Dairy House, at one time owned by Dudley, Earl of Leicester. George III purchased the Dutch House in 1781 as an annexe to his main Kew residence — the White House, which lay to the south on a site now marked by a sundial (see 9). This annexe served as an occasional nursery for his fifteen children, including the Prince of Wales and the Duke of York. In 1802 the White House was pulled down and the Dutch House became the King's Kew residence. Later, in ill health, he moved out to Windsor, but Queen Charlotte continued to occupy Kew Palace from time to time until her death there in 1818. The interior view (12) shows Queen Charlotte's Bedchamber. The Queen's Garden, at the back of the palace (11 and 13), is laid out in 17th century style and features a parterre, nosegay garden and pleached alley of *Laburnum*. The building is open to the public in the summer months.

'I would give 3/6 for it — as its cracked accross [sic]'

KEW PALACE.

8

KEW PALACE.

4/8/05

9

Kew Gardens.—Kew Palace.   58

10

11

17

12

13

'No. P.22 Crown Copyright'

18

The Temple of the Sun

The Temple of the Sun, erected by Sir William Chambers, is sadly no longer to be seen. It used to stand between the Orangery and the T-Range until on 28 March 1916, during a violent storm, a large cedar of Lebanon fell on and demolished it. As it was constructed of lath and plaster and not of solid stone the damage was quite irreparable and a maidenhair tree *(Ginkgo biloba)* planted by Queen Mary in 1923 now stands on the site.

'Do you object to these instead of letter—I thought two might answer the same purpose'

14

15 KEW GARDENS. SUN TEMPLE

13106   Temple of the Sun, Kew Gardens.

16

Stone Pine

One of the oldest exotic trees at Kew is the elegant Stone Pine *(Pinus pinea)*, a native of the Mediterranean and a characteristic species of Italian landscapes. It is sited near the private grounds at the back of the director's office, and has edible seeds.

17

Cambridge Cottage

The Wood Museum (or Museum No 4) is part of Cambridge Cottage, originally the residence of the Dukes of Cambridge. Queen Mary spent much of her girlhood in the cottage and its grounds. After the death of the last duke the house and gardens were presented to Kew by King Edward VII. The attractive walled garden has been kept, as far as possible, as an old-fashioned flower garden. The main building was opened to the public in 1910 as the Museum of British Forestry but later, in 1957, became a general wood and timber museum with special emphasis on Commonwealth timbers.

'Series No. 3. K. 18'

Bordering the south-facing wall of Cambridge Cottage Garden is the Duchess' Border (formerly known as the Duchess' Walk). Exotic shrubs and climbers planted along the wall survive even the most bleak of English winters.

The Duchess' Walk, Kew Gardens.

The Rock Garden

The Rock Garden, best visited in early summer, was constructed in 1882 during the regime of Sir Joseph Hooker, for the reception of a collection of herbaceous plants (mainly alpines) presented by the executors of George C Joad of Wimbledon. It was intended to reproduce the rocky course of a Pyrenean stream, with

'Went to Kew yesterday—it was simply lovely'

18099   THE DRIPPING WELL, KEW GARDENS   PHOTO. GALE & POLDEN. LTD.

20

the 157 metres long path representing the stream bed, a design which has not always been consistently followed. The principal rock used in the original landscaping was Cheddar limestone, but this has been largely replaced with Sussex sandstone which holds water better and heats up less. The modern Alpine House, close to the Jodrell Laboratory, was opened in 1981 and should not be missed.

From an original
watercolour by C T Howard

Visitors are not permitted to
remain at Kew after dark so
this presents a scene that
you will not otherwise see!

The Dripping Well forms
part of the watercourse in
the Rock Garden

23

The Rose Pergola

Dividing the herbaceous or 'order' beds is the Rose Pergola (card 24). The plants in the order beds are arranged in families, following the classification of Bentham and Hooker, and are ideal for teaching students of botany.

24

The Rose Pergola, Kew Gardens.

T-Range glasshouses

In addition to the famous Palm and Temperate Houses there have been many lesser-known glasshouses at Kew, some of which still stand today. Houses numbered 7 to 14 constituted the 'T-range', so named because of their combined shape (slightly altered by later additions). They were all removed to make way for the Princess of Wales Conservatory, opened in July 1987. Greenhouse No 4 (25) was the original Conservatory devoted to the display of flowers in season: card 26 shows one of the orchid houses that formed part of the T-range complex.

25 KEW GARDENS, GREENHOUSE. No. 4   50216

One of the Orchid Houses, Kew Gardens.

26

House No 10 at the centre of the T-range was the Water Lily House, later known as the Victoria Amazonica House, and famous for its yearly display of the Giant Amazon Water Lily (formerly *V. regia* after Queen Victoria, as seen on the Tuck 'Oilette' card, 27). Card 64 of R S & Co (card 28 in this book), is erroneously labelled 'Orchid House'. It too illustrates House 10 in the days when *Victoria amazonica* was cultivated in House No 15, a small hothouse to the north of the Palm House.

"OILETTE"

'"Oilette" (Regd.) Postcard 7562'

27 KEW GARDENS. VICTORIA REGIA HOUSE.

Kew Gardens—Orchid House. 64

28

'Hope you are quite well and not feeling very dull'

26

Victoria amazonica

Victoria amazonica produces giant leaves that can reach six feet in diameter and support a small child. It first flowered at Kew in 1850. The flowers, produced in summer, open in the evening and are pure white, but fade to pink or purple within 24 hours. The species is still grown in the Princess of Wales Conservatory, where it is one of the star attractions.

'With best wishes for Christmas and the New Year'

29

30

Princess of Wales Conservatory

The Princess of Wales Conservatory was opened by the Princess of Wales in July 1987. It is a masterpiece of modern design and technology providing ten different climatic zones for a range of tropical and subtropical plants. It includes a collection of cacti from the Sherman Hoyt Cactus House (No 7A of the old T-range), some of which are shown here in their original setting. In the background is a painted scene of the Mohave Desert.

31

32

The Temple of Aeolus

Beside Cumberland Gate a wild garden covers part of an artificial mound sur-mounted by the Temple of Aeolus. The temple was erected by Sir William Chambers about 1761 and was rebuilt to its original design (a hemispherical dome supported by eight columns) by Decimus Burton in 1845, on the instruc-tion of Sir William Hooker. The area is particularly attractive in spring when thousands of daffodils are in bloom.

TEMPLE OF AEOLUS,
KEW GARDENS.

33

'It is just too good of you to think so much for me, and I am more than grateful'

'"Garden and Floral" Series'
'An Entirely British
Production'

MAGNOLIA BLOSSOM AND YELLOW DAFFODILS IN THE 'DELL'
AT KEW.

34

The Museum

The General Museum (or Museum No 1), situated on the east side of the Pond opposite the Palm House, was designed by Decimus Burton and erected in 1856. It was initially used as a museum of economic botany but today houses other exhibits as well. In 1880 the whole of the collections of the Indian Museum, South Kensington, were transferred to the east wing of the museum — specially built to house the collection, and paid for by the Indian Government. The Pond between the museum and the Palm House is all that remains of the great lake of George III's day which covered an area now occupied by the Palm House, Rose Garden and beyond.

The Museum, Kew Gardens.

35

Rob Hughes

LONDON. IN KEW GARDENS.

Very many thanks for your pretty postcard. Hope you will like this one. F. H.

'Raphael Tuck & Sons'
"County" Postcard Series
504 XII. "London"'

36

By Appointment

'Just a line to let you know I am still alive'
'"Oilette" (Regd.) Postcard
7562'

KEW GARDENS, MUSEUM AND POND

37

38

One of the original exhibits, displaying various plants and plant products of economic importance. The cabinet on the left contains cotton

39

The Palm House

The finest of its kind in Europe, Kew's Palm House was built essentially to the design of Decimus Burton. Construction of this beautiful glasshouse, 110.3 metres long and 20.1 metres high, commenced in 1844 and was completed in 1848. Nearly five miles of hot-water pipes were installed to keep the palms, cycads and other tropical plants at the required temperature. The Palm House was completely restored in 1958 and has recently undergone more massive renovation work. After replanting, it should reopen to the public in early 1990.

'We found some mushrooms yesterday, it was a treat for us'
'Series 101-106'

40

KEW GARDENS. The Palm House and Lake.

London — The Palm House Kew Gardens

No. 6179

41

From an original watercolour by C T Howard

A view with the holly hedge surrounding the rose garden seen mid-distance

'Many Happy Returns of the Day'

'No. P. 7 Crown Copyright'

42 KEW GARDENS. The PALM HOUSE

THE PALM HOUSE KEW GARDENS.

43

44

Two similar interior views
of the Palm House showing
the South African cycad,
Encephalartus altensteinii,
with, on the more recent
colour postcard, its golden
female cones, flanked by
the mauve-flowered
Brunfelsia calycina and
several variegated Crotons

45

46

47

'No. P. 12 Crown Copyright'

A Palm House promenade concert firework finale

Printed
iu
Saxony.

Inside the Palm House—a colourwashed card showing elegant palms, cycads and climbers

48

Kew Gardens,
Interior of the Palm House.

49

36

The Rose Garden

The Rose Garden lies to the west of the Palm House and is enclosed by a large holly hedge. Wrongly labelled, card 51 illustrates the Rose Garden in its early days when it was planted with herbaceous plants. The American Gardens, made by Sir William Hooker in the early 1850s, contained many plants introduced from North America, and lay to the west of the Rose Garden on a site later replanted with Azaleas after remodelling and enlargement by Sir Joseph Hooker in 1881. The Palm House was used by the 19th century landscape architect Nesfield as a focal point for various vistas—Syon Vista runs to the River Thames, bisecting the Rose Garden on route, and the one illustrated here leads the eye southwards to the Pagoda.

'"We have to gain the Victory. That is our task." —The Prime Minister'

POST CARD

Affix
1/2 d. Stamp
Inland

1 d. Stamp
Foreign

ROSE GARDEN. KEW GARDENS.

50

22270 Kew Gardens. American Gardens.

51

The Rhododendron Dell

The Rhododendron Dell, formerly called 'Hollow Walk', was constructed in 1773, supposedly by the Staffordshire Militia when quartered at Kew, for the Dowager Princess of Wales (mother of George III). The walk was almost certainly designed by 'Capability' Brown and was later planted with Rhododendrons, mostly from Western China and Tibet, by Sir William Hooker. Today the Dell includes many modern hybrids together with some of their parent species and is a blaze of colour from mid May to early June.

'Its very warm today & rather dull now after a lovely morning'

'Will be over on Friday night after tea'

RHODODENDRON WALK, KEW GARDENS.

52

THE RHODODENDRON WALK KEW GARDENS

53

The Rhododendron Dell, Kew Gardens.

54

The Lake and the Lily Pond

The Lake, to the south of Syon Vista, (not to be confused with the Pond situated between the Palm House and Museum No 1) covers about four and a half acres and is entirely artificial. It was largely excavated between 1857 and 1861 and much of the material removed was used to lay out some 24-26 kilometres of pathway in the gardens. In about 1859 a further large quantity of gravel was dug out to build the terrace on which the Temperate House now stands. The Lake is connected by an underground culvert to the Thames from which it can be topped-up at high tide. There are four islands in the centre on which several ornamental wildfowl breed.

The Lake, Kew Gardens.

'C. W. Faulkner & Co...Series No. 527F'

55

40

56

KEW GARDENS. The LAKE

57

MAYTIME. THE LAKE
KEW GARDENS

58

V 4668   KEW GARDENS, THE LAKESIDE.

Kew's wildfowl collection is constantly changing but there are always several ornamental waterbirds to be seen on the Lake and Pond. The Mandarins and Carolinas illustrated on the Clarke & Sherwell card (59) frequent the Pond in front of Museum No 1 and breed freely in the gardens. Some of the birds were gifts and others were exchanged for tropical plants used to enhance the displays in the reptile houses at London Zoo. Just like some of the rare plants at Kew, the birds have had to put up with the attentions of the occasional unscrupulous visitor. In the early 1970s eggs were stolen from a Black Swan's nest on one of the islets in the centre of the Lake. It is also rumoured that one hungry visitor was caught redhanded attempting to leave the gardens with a duck under his jacket — presumably destined for Sunday lunch!

(a) *Mandarins*   (b) *Carolinas*

ROYAL BOTANIC GARDENS, KEW

59   97.   Produced by Clarke & Sherwell Ltd.   60

The Water Lily Pond, Kew Gardens.

An old gravel pit near the Queen's Cottage grounds was transformed into a waterlily pond in 1897 and devoted to the cultivation of various water-loving plants. A deciduous Mississippi Swamp Cypress *(Taxodium distichum)* is one of the elegant trees growing in the pond

The Queen's Cottage

The Queen's Cottage was built by George III for Queen Charlotte, probably in the early 1770s, for royal picnics. Together with its 37 acres of woodland it was given to the gardens, as a Diamond Jubilee gift, by Queen Victoria. Picturesque and romantic though it is, the cottage has no water, light or sanitary fittings. Upholding Queen Victoria's official request, the grounds are kept in a semi-wild state and are best seen in late spring when the carpets of bluebells are a joy to behold.

Stengel & Co., Dresden — Berlin 8481

Queens Cottage

Kew

Please tell Oliv that W.W.B. address is 58 Linden Gardens, Chiswick. I think Miss Seare has returned to Richmond. — Isn't this a pretty picture? G.S.

6 Sept. 1902.

61

225   KEW GARDENS (Near London). — Queen's Cottage. — LL.

62

63

'I am glad to say that up to now we are all safe and well' (16 July 1944)

64

65

66

The Picnic Room in the
cottage: sadly, visitors are
not permitted to take tea
here

67

The Japanese Gateway

About 120 metres to the west of the Pagoda is a small mound, on the summit of which stands a replica of a famous Japanese gate, 'The Gateway of the Imperial Messenger' or 'Chokushi-Mon'. This was one of the exhibits shown at the Japanese Exhibition at Shepherd's Bush in 1910, and was presented to the gardens by the Kyoto Exhibitors' Association at the close of the exhibition. The beautiful structure, built mainly of *Cupressus obtusa,* is notable for the exquisite delicacy of its carving. The mound is called Mosque or 'Moss' Hill (the latter doubtless a corruption), as at one time there stood another of Sir William Chambers' buildings, the Mosque, which was demolished or fell into decay early in the 19th century.

KEW GARDENS
The JAPANESE GATEWAY

From an original watercolour by C T Howard 'If sent at Printed Matter Rate the words Post Card Must be Struck Out.'

68

Japanese Temple, Kew Gardens

69

46

70

The Pagoda

The Pagoda, 49.7 metres high and built in 1761–62 to the design of Sir William Chambers, remains one of the landmarks of the gardens. Octagonal in shape and ten storeys high it must have been spectacular in its day, as each corner of each roof was originally adorned with a multicoloured, varnished dragon with a bell in its mouth. Extensive repair work was carried out sometime between 1820 and 1840 and the building subsequently withstood the explosions of seven German bombs, which fell around it in 1941. During the same period planks were removed from the various landings so that experiments in ballistics could be carried out. The Pagoda is not open to the public.

TRADE MARK

"OILETTE"

'"Oilette" (Regd.) Postcard 7562'

71 KEW GARDENS. THE PAGODA

'Valentine's Series'

The Pagoda, Kew Gardens

Kew Gardens, Pagoda   Kew

72

73

74

75

76

'Valentines Series'

The Restaurant and the Ruined Arch

'The most delightful spot in which one could possibly take tea on a summer afternoon': the Refreshment Pavilion, southeast of the Temperate House, was burnt down by suffragettes in 1913 but rebuilt in 1915. It closes during the winter months.

'Visited everything of importance amongst the sights, this place included'

THE REFRESHMENT PAVILION.
KEW GARDENS.

77

The Ruined Arch, just south of the Marianne North Gallery, was designed by Sir William Chambers to imitate a Roman antiquity. Built in 1759-60, it also served the practical function of supporting a carriageway from Kew Road into the gardens. The arch is built of brick with a stone façade, but the latter has slowly crumbled away to leave the arch more ruined than ever.

78

'Series No. 1. K. 3'

The Marianne North Gallery

The remarkable Victorian artist and traveller, Miss Marianne North, presented her 832 paintings of trees, flowers and landscapes, together with the building in which to house them, to the nation in the late 19th century. The gallery opened to the public in 1882. Cards 81-83, all modern, show three of her paintings.

79

'No. P. N. 33 Crown
Copyright'

80

Painting No 230
View from Rangaroon,
near Darjeeling, India

81

Painting No 684
Foliage, flowers and fruit
of the Sacred Lotus,
Nelumbo nucifera, Java

82

'MN. 5 Crown Copyright'

Painting No 658
Distant view of Mount
Fujiyama, Japan, and
Wisteria

83

The Flagstaff

Over the years four flagstaffs have been presented to Kew. The first, 36 metres high, was cut in two by a tug boat while being towed up the River Thames from London Docks. The two pieces were spliced together but the pole and its hoisting equipment blew down in a violent storm and it broke into three. A second flagpole, 48.5 metres high, was eventually erected in 1861 but was replaced in 1919 by this one, 65 metres high, presented by the government of British Colombia. In 1957 it was discovered that the pole's top had been attacked by a wood-rotting fungus and 25.6 metres of it had to be removed. The present flagstaff, a fine shaped trunk of Douglas Fir *(Pseudotsuga menziesii)*, is 68.6 metres high and about 370 years old. It was presented to Kew in 1958 to celebrate British Colombia's centenary, and was erected by the 23rd Field Squadron of the Royal Engineers on 5 November 1959. Not one centimetre of the flagstaff is buried in the ground — it is pivoted over a concrete inspection chamber and held in position by several metal hawsers.

84

The Temperate House

Designed by Decimus Burton and built between 1860 and 1898, the Temperate House covers an area of $1\frac{3}{8}$ acres — more than three times the size of the great Conservatory at Chatsworth. Once known as the Winter Garden, this magnificent glasshouse is devoted to the cultivation of plants unable to tolerate our English winters if grown outside. After restoration work, it was formally reopened by Queen Elizabeth II in 1982.

85 KEW GARDENS   THE TEMPERATE HOUSE & THE PAGODA

3100

86

The Temperate House, or Winter Garden, Kew.

Palms and tree ferns from Australasia and South America growing in the central section of the Temperate House. Postcard 88 is undated, but is certainly pre-Second World War

87

88

89

King William's Temple

King William's Temple is the only monument at Kew that was built during the reign of King William IV. It was erected in 1837 to the design of Jeffrey Wyatville. The two statues are by Pietro Francavilla, born in Cambrai, France in 1548: they were removed in the late 1950s and used to enhance the interior of the Orangery. They are now on permanent loan to the Victoria and Albert Museum. At one time the temple contained a number of busts of the royal family but these have long since been removed to Windsor. At present the only interior decoration is a series of plaques around the walls enumerating the battles fought by the British Army between 1760 and 1815.

'This space may be used for communication for Inland Postage and Foreign Countries, except Japan, Spain, and United States'

90   *Kew Gardens—King William's Temple.*   71

The Herbarium

The Herbarium and Library, situated 100 yards to the right of the main gates, are not open to the public and most visitors to Kew probably pass them by without a second glance. But the Herbarium houses one of the world's greatest collections of dried plant specimens, systematically arranged by plant family, genus and species, and the library boasts the best collection of botanical books anywhere.

Every day, from all over the world, botanists come to study in this Mecca of plant identification and classification. The original building was purchased by the Crown from Robert Hunter in 1818, but was not used as a herbarium until 1852. The extensive collections of George Bentham and Sir William Hooker, which form the main basis of the present collections, were added in 1854 and 1867 respectively. As the collections expanded, new buildings were added to house them in 1877, 1902, 1932 and 1969. Nobody knows just how many specimens there are but it could be close to six million. A new unit (topped by a rather incongruous Buddhist garden) designed to hold a further one million plants has recently been built in the central quadrangle.

91

Inside 'Wing C' (built in 1877) – those who have seen pictures of English prisons may recognise some similarities!

92

Spring flowers

'Kew Gardens in Springtime'—two Tuck 'Oilettes' from original paintings by M Townsend. Above, a bank of crocuses and below, cherry blossom with a holly hedge and the Palm House just visible in the distance.

The official caption on the reverse of the crocuses reads: 'The beauty of these Gardens cannot be imagined except by those who visit them in Spring and Summertime. Wild flowers and woodland, blossoming trees and vernal glades, leafy avenues and exotic plants in green-houses, beauties of every sort to suit all tastes and give delight to all comers'.

'We all had a great day yesterday'
'"Oilette" Postcard No. 3647'

By Appointment

"OILETTE"

'"Oilette" Postcard No. 3647'

93

94

'Gold Framed Post Cards. Regd. Copyright Series No. 3 Nature's Gardens'

95

Daffodils, and flowering cherries from Japan. The latter were first widely planted in England in the early 20th century

96

'No. 48'

A glimpse of the Thames through a bluebell wood

'Surrey. Series No. 39 ...Painted by Sutton Palmer, described by A. R. Hope Moncrieff'

A carpet of bluebells in springtime

'Gold Framed Post Cards. Regd. Copyright Series No 3 Nature's Gardens'

97

98

99

℗lant portraits

Rhododendron nobleanum Lindl.
ROYAL BOTANIC GARDENS, KEW.
42.
Produced by W. F. Sedgwick, Limited
100

Rhododendron arboreum Sm.
ROYAL BOTANIC GARDENS, KEW.
40.
Produced by W. F. Sedgwick, Limited
101

Rhododendron nobleanum
(= *Rhododendron* x
pulcherrimum)

Three species of *Sarracenia*
and a *Darlingtonia*, all
insectivorous plants:
(a) *S. flava* is more
probably a hybrid involving
S. flava & perhaps
S. purpurea;
(b) *S. drumondii* is a
synonym of *S. leucophylla*
and (d) *S. illustrata* is *S.* x
mitchelliana

102

SARRACENIAS
(a) *S. flava*   (b) *S. Drummondii*
(c) *S. illustrata*   (d) *Darlingtonia californica*
ROYAL BOTANIC GARDENS, KEW.
Produced by Clarke & Sherwell Ltd.
1

Cyclamen coum

Strelitzia reginae

Dendrobium thyrsiflorum
— an orchid

103

Cyclamen coum Mill.
ROYAL BOTANIC GARDENS, KEW.

Produced by W. F. Sedgwick, Limited

33.

56

104

Strelitzia reginae Ait.
ROYAL BOTANIC GARDENS, KEW.

Produced by Clarke & Sherwell Ltd.

105

Dendrobium thyrsiflorum Rchb. f.
ROYAL BOTANIC GARDENS, KEW.

Produced by W. F. Sedgwick, Limited

106.

Agave atrovirens, in the Amaryllidaceae, yields pulque, the national drink of Mexico. Agaves became known as Century Plants because of the erroneous impression that they took 100 years to flower: some species flower in eight years, and even the larger ones do so in 30 to 40 years. After flowering and fruiting the plant then dies. From some species sisal is extracted to make a useful thread

'Series No. 3 K.13.'

106

Kew

The road from Kew Bridge towards the main gates, with Kew Green to the left of the picture. Several teashops and restaurants evidently catered for many visitors to Kew even though there is little activity on this early photograph!

'The "Wyndham" Series'

107

THE "WYNDHAM" SERIES.

A view from the top end of Kew Road, with Kew Church hidden by trees on the left and the tramlines heading off into the distance in the direction of Kew Bridge. The card was posted in October 1905

'I should be very pleased to see you any day you can come over'

108

Kew Road and Victoria Gate—still the most convenient entrance for visitors arriving by London Underground

'The "Darlow" Series. No. 1509'

109

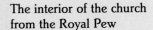
Kew parish church (St Anne's) and the green where cricket is still played in the summer months

'The "Wyndham" Series'

110

St Anne's church from the front. The graveyard is of interest to botanists as Sir William Aiton and his son and Sir William and Sir Joseph Hooker are all buried there. Two noted artists were also interred at St Anne's—Thomas Gainsborough's tomb is on the south side of the church and that of Johan Zoffany on the east

'I should love to go with you to "Henry of Navarre" on Wed.'

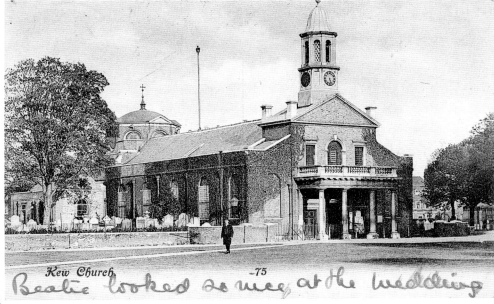

111

The interior of the church from the Royal Pew

'With every wish that this and every Easter may be a very happy one'

112

Kew Bridge and the Thames

Kew Bridge was rebuilt between 1899 and 1903, and officially reopened by King Edward VII on 20 May 1903. The gaslights have long since gone — removed during the Second World War to be melted down and perhaps remoulded into military equipment

'We shall be charmed to see you'

Kew Bridge.

113

Kew Bridge.

114

'Keep this card and all the others I will send you as I want to get the set...This is not the boat that got stuck in the mud'

"OILETTE"

Kew Bridge from Strand-on-the-Green

'"Oilette" (Regd.) Postcard 7127..."Picturesque Counties" – Middlesex. Series 1'

King Edward VII. Bridge,   (Kew).

115

KEW BRIDGE.

116

Two delightful scenes of the
River Thames at Kew

'"Oilette" Postcard 8546
"Up the River"'

'C.W. Faulkner & Co. Ltd.
London, E.C. Series 1271'

117

118   Kew.

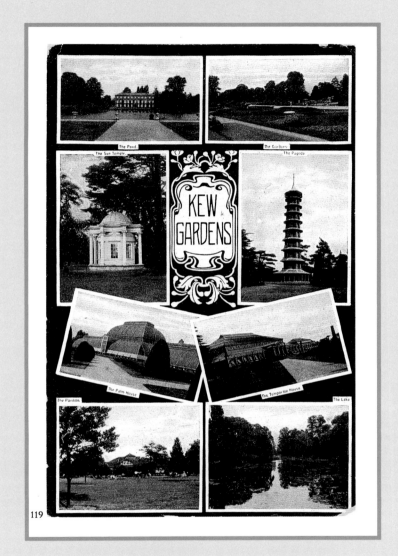

'We will be very pleased to come over on Sunday next if fine'
'No. 133 Copyright Chaucer Postcard Publishing'
Postmarked 22 October 1919

119

Appendix

Firms that printed and published most of the cards illustrated in the book:

A C Black Ltd (Soho Square, London) 98
C W Faulkner & Co Ltd (London) 55, 118
Charles Martin (Aldermanbury, London) 9
Chaucer Postcard Publishing Co (Railton Road, Herne Hill, London) 119
Clarke & Sherwell Ltd 59, 97, 102, 104
Davidson Bros (London & New York) 115
G D & D (London) 6
Gale & Polden Ltd (London, Aldershot & Portsmouth) 1, 8, 16, 18, 19, 20, 24, 26, 35, 43, 45, 53, 54, 60, 65, 73, 77, 78, 86, 106
Harvey Barton & Son Ltd (Bristol) 58
J Arthur Dixon Ltd 46, 89
J Salmon Ltd (Sevenoaks) 21, 33, 42, 50, 52, 56, 57, 63, 64, 68, 76, 85
Misch & Co's 'Camera Graphs' 5
Photochrom Co Ltd (London & Tunbridge Wells) 25
R S & Co (Old Street, London) 10, 28, 90, 111
Raphael Tuck & Sons 3, 15, 27, 36, 37, 71, 93, 94, 116, 117
S Hildesheimer & Co Ltd (London & Manchester, printed in Saxony) 22
Stengel & Co (Redcross Street, London, printed in Dresden) 61, 74
Tester Massey & Co Ltd 95, 99
The Campfield Press (St Albans) — for HMSO 12
W F Sedgwick Ltd 100, 101, 103, 105
W S Cowell Ltd (Crown copyright) 96
W T Cook Ltd (Caterham) 17, 29
Willsons Printers (Leicester) Ltd — for HMSO 7, 13, 44, 47, 67, 70, 80, 83

References

A Vision of Eden, the Life and Work of Marianne North, Webb & Bower, 1980
Bean, W J, *The Royal Botanic Gardens, Kew: Historical and Descriptive,* Cassell & Co Ltd, 1908
Blunt, W, *In for a Penny — a prospect of Kew,* Hamish Hamilton, 1978
Dûval, W & Monahan, V, *Collecting Postcards in Colour, 1894-1914,* Blandford Press, 1979
Hepper, F N (ed), *Royal Botanic Gardens, Kew — Gardens for Science and Pleasure,* HMSO, 1982
Holt, T & Holt, V, *Picture Postcard Artists — Landscapes, Animals & Characters,* Longman, 1984
King, R, *The World of Kew,* Macmillan, 1976
Popular Official Guide to the Royal Botanic Gardens, Kew, HMSO, 1921
The Royal Botanic Gardens, Kew — an illustrated guide, HMSO, 1961
Turrill, W B, *Royal Botanic Gardens, Kew, Past and Present,* Herbert Jenkins, 1959
Wallis, E J, *The Royal Botanic Gardens, Kew,* Effingham Wilson, 1900

Printed in the United Kingdom for Her Majesty's Stationery Office Dd 289371 C350 4/89.